CONTENTS.

1. Home-made Yeast and the first Loaf
2. Bread Sponge and Breakfast Breads
3. Breakfast Breads
4. Other Breakfast Breads
5. Eggs
6. Broiled Meats
7. Fried Meats
8. What to do with Left-overs
9. Other Dinner Dishes
10. Meats
11. Vegetables
12. Desserts
13. Cake-making

1
HOME-MADE YEAST AND THE FIRST LOAF.

THE question is often asked, "What is the most important branch of culinary knowledge? What the chief requisite in supplying the table well and healthfully?"

The experienced housewife cannot hesitate as to the reply.

Beyond doubt, the ability to make *good* bread. No one need rise hungry from a table on which is plenty of light, sweet bread, white or brown, and good butter. For the latter item many of us are dependent upon market and grocery. It is hardly just to hold the cook responsible for imperfections in this regard when she has bought the best articles these supply. She is culpable if she fails to see that her board furnishes three times a day a bountiful allowance of what I hope none of my friends in council will ever call "*healthy* bread." The eater may be made or kept healthy by the consumption of nutritious, wholesome, healthful or healthsome food; but the most careful philologists do not speak of edibles as subject to such diseases as may afflict living creatures.

While it is always wise to use none except the best flour in bread-making, it is true that skilful management of an inferior brand will often produce better loaves and biscuits than careless treatment of fine family flour. I say this that none may be discouraged. So far as my observation and experience extend, nothing can remedy the disadvantage of indifferent yeast.

Let me earnestly advise, therefore, as the foundation of successful baking, the manufacture of

HOME-MADE YEAST.

Four large mealy potatoes, peeled.

Two quarts of cold water.

One teacupful of loose, dry hops, *or*, half a cake of the pressed hops put up by the Shakers and sold by druggists.

Two tablespoonfuls of white sugar.

Four tablespoonfuls of flour.

Half a cupful lively yeast, *or* a yeast-cake dissolved in a little warm water.

Put water, potatoes, and the hops tied up in a bit of coarse muslin, over the fire in a clean pot or kettle. Boil until the potatoes break apart when a fork is stuck into them. Unless they are very old or very new, this should be half an hour after the boiling begins. Take out the potatoes, leaving water and hops on the range where they will boil slowly. Mash the potatoes smooth in a wooden tray or large crockery bowl, with a wooden spoon, and work in the sugar. When these are well-mixed wet the paste with three tablespoonfuls of the boiling hop-tea, then stir in a tablespoonful of flour. Do this four times, beating and stirring to get rid of lumps. When the flour is all in, add, a little at a time, the rest of the hop-tea, squeezing the bag hard to get every drop. Throw the boiled hops away, and wash the cloth or bag well before putting it aside for the next yeast-making.

Strain the thick, grayish liquid through a colander into a bowl and let it get almost but not quite cold before you stir in the half cupful of made yeast that is to "raise" it. Set aside out of the dust and wind, put a sieve or throw a bit of mosquito netting over it, and leave it to work. It is a good plan to set the bowl in a large pan or dish to catch what may run over the sides. When the yeast ceases to sing or hiss, and the bubbles no longer rise and break on the surface, the fermentation is complete. Four or five hours in July, seven in January, usually bring this to pass. Pour the yeast into glass fruit-jars with close covers, or stone-jars fitted with corks, or common bottles, tying the corks down with twine. Keep in a *cool*, dark place, and do not open except to draw off the quantity needed for a baking. In the refrigerator it will keep good for a month. Shake up the bottle before pouring out what you want into a cup.

The creamy, foamy product thus obtained is quite another thing from the dark, bitter stuff pedled from one kitchen door to another as brewer's or baker's yeast, unfit for use unless strained, and then too frequently "unprofitable" because "stale" and "flat."

THE FIRST LOAF.

One quart and a cupful of sifted flour (a half pint cup)

One even teaspoonful dry salt.

Two full cups of blood-warm water.

Five tablespoonfuls of yeast (good ones).

Sift the flour and salt together into a wooden or stoneware bowl. Make a hole in the middle and pour in the yeast, then a cupful of the water. With clean hands begin to work down the flour into the liquid, and as it stiffens add the rest of the water. When the dough is all wet dust your fingers with dry flour, and rub off the paste into the bowl. Scrape the sides of this, dust your fingers again, and make all the dough into a lump or ball. Dredge your pastry or bread-board well with flour, put the dough upon it and sift flour lightly over it. Ask your mother or some experienced person whether or not it is of the right consistency. There is so much difference in various brands of flour that only practice can teach one when the dough is just right. *Do not get it too stiff.* Add flour very cautiously even should it stick to your fingers. Knead the bread for fifteen minutes—not so fast as to tire yourself out of breath, but steadily and hard, working it away from you all the time, turning the ball over and around so as to reach every part of the mass. It should leave the board without stickiness at the end of this time, be smooth, firm, and elastic. Strike it hard with a tight fist, and if the dent thus made fills up at once, you have kneaded it sufficiently.

Sprinkle your bread-bowl with flour, put the dough in the bottom, sift flour lightly over the top, cover with a clean thick cloth and set, in cold weather, in a moderately warm place, in summer, out of the draught, but away from the fire and sun. It should be light in four hours in warm weather, in six in winter. If you wish to have it for breakfast, set at bedtime, and get up early to work it over for the second rising.

This must not be done until the dough has swollen immensely, and cracked over the top like "crazed" china. Flour the board and knead as before, now for ten minutes. Grease two "brick" or round bread-pans well with sweet lard or butter, make out the dough in two oblong or round loaves, and pat these down in the pans to fit the corners. Prick the tops with a sharp fork, cover with a clean cloth, and let them stand for an hour before putting them into the oven.

The oven must be steady, but not too hot. You should be able to hold your bare arm in it while you count twenty regularly. Should the bread rise very fast at first, lay stout paper over the top to prevent it from browning before the heart is done. Do not allow the stove or range to be filled with fresh coal or wood while your bread is in the oven, or it will be "slack-baked." Should you need to increase the heat, put in a stick or two of wood to get up a brisk blaze. Do not open the oven for ten or twelve minutes after the bread goes in, and very seldom afterward. A peep should suffice to see how it is getting on. If the loaf rises higher at the back or at one side than in front or on the other side, turn the tin quickly, and do not jar it, or it will "fall" into heavy streaks. If the oven is right, your loaves should be done in *about* thirty-five minutes.

Set the loaves up on the edge of one end, leaning against the wall or an upright board, that the air may dry the bottom, throw a dry cloth over them and leave them to cool. When quite cold wrap in a clean thick cloth and keep in a tin box or stone crock.

In this, as in other first attempts, let me warn you against being disheartened by failure, partial or total. It would be far more strange were you to accomplish perfection in one, or in half a dozen lessons, than if your early efforts should be only moderately successful.

See that your yeast is lively and not sour, the flour good and dry, then follow directions implicitly, and I think I can engage that the result will not mortify you.

2
BREAD SPONGE AND BREAKFAST BREADS.

BREAD raised with what is known to bakers as a "sponge," requires more time and a trifle more work than the simpler form for which I have just already given directions. But it keeps fresh longer, is softer and more nutritious, and a second-rate brand of flour thus treated produces a better loaf than when mixed up with yeast and water only. Sponge-making is, therefore, an important if not an essential accomplishment in a cook, be she novice or veteran.

Bread Sponge.

> Three potatoes of fair size, peeled and boiled mealy.
>
> Five tablespoonfuls of yeast.
>
> One tablespoonful of white sugar.
>
> One tablespoonful of butter.
>
> Three cups of lukewarm water in which the potatoes were boiled—strained through a coarse cloth.
>
> One heaping cup of sifted flour.

Put the potatoes into a large bowl or tray and mash them to powder with a potato beetle, or a wooden spoon. While still hot, mix in the sugar and butter, beating all to a lumpless cream.

Add a *few* spoonfuls at a time, the potato-water alternately with the flour by the handful, beating the batter smooth as you go on until all of the liquid and flour has gone in. Beat hard one minute before pouring in the yeast. In hot weather, it is well to stir into the yeast a bit of soda no larger than a grain of corn already wet up in a teaspoonful of boiling water.

Now whip up the batter with a wooden spoon for another minute, and the sponge is made.

Throw a cloth over the bowl and set by for five or six hours to rise. If you intend to bake in the forenoon, make the sponge at bedtime. If in the afternoon, early in the morning.

When the sponge is light sift a quart and a cup of flour into a bowl or tray with two teaspoonfuls of salt. Into a hollow, like a crater in the middle of the flour, empty your sponge-bowl, and work the flour down into it. Wash out the bowl with a little lukewarm water and add this to the dough. If it should prove too soft, work in, cautiously, a little more flour. If too stiff, warm water, a spoonful at a time until you can handle the paste easily. *The danger is in getting it too stiff.*

Now, knead and set for risings first and second, as you have already been instructed. This sponge will be found especially useful in making

Graham Bread.

One quart of Graham flour, one cup of white flour.

One half cup of Indian meal.

One half cup of molasses.

Two teaspoonfuls of salt.

Soda, the size of a pea.

Half the quantity of sponge given in preceding receipt.

Warm water for rinsing bowl—about half a cup.

Put the brown or Graham flour *unsifted* into the bread-bowl. Sift into it white flour, meal and salt, and stir up well while dry. Into the "crater" dug out in the middle, pour the sponge, warm water, the molasses, and soda dissolved in hot water. Knead as you would white bread, and set aside for the rising. It will not swell so fast as the white, so give yourself more time for making it.

When light, knead well and long; make into two loaves, then put into well-greased pans and leave for an hour, or until it becomes more than twice the original size of the dough.

Take care that it does not burn in baking. The molasses renders it liable to scorching. The oven must be steady, but not so hot as for white bread, nor will the Graham bread be done quite so soon as that made of bolted flour. Turn the pans once while baking, moving them as gently as possible. If rudely shaken or jarred, there will be heavy streaks in the loaves.

Graham bread is wholesome and sweet, and ought to be eaten frequently in every family, particularly by young people whose bones and teeth are in forming.

The phosphates which the process of "bolting" removes to a large extent from white flour, go directly to the manufacture of bone, and these also tend to nourish and strengthen the brain.

Tea-Rolls.

After mixing your bread in the morning either with sponge or with yeast, divide the kneaded dough into two portions. Mould one into a round ball, and set aside for a loaf as already directed. Make a hole in the middle of the other batch and pour into it a tablespoonful of butter, just melted, but not hot. Close the dough over it, dust your hands and kneading-board with flour and work in the shortening until the dough is elastic and ceases to be sticky. Put it into a floured bowl, cover with a cloth and set away out of draught and undue heat, for three hours. Knead it again, then, and wait upon its rising for another three hours. The dough should be as soft as can be handled.

When it is light for the second time flour your board, rubbing in the flour and blowing lightly away what does not adhere to the surface. Toss the lump dough upon it and knead thoroughly for five minutes. Flour a rolling-pin and roll the dough into a sheet not more than half an inch thick. Cut this into round cakes with a biscuit-cutter or a sharp-edged tumbler and fold, not quite in the middle, in the form of turnovers, pinching the corners of the fold pretty hard to hinder the flap of dough from flying up as the rising proceeds. Rub the bottom and sides of a baking-pan with sweet lard or butter. Do this with a bit of clean soft rag or tissue-paper, visiting every corner of the pan, but not leaving thick layers and streaks of grease after it. Arrange the rolls in regular rows in the pan about a quarter of an inch apart.

Cover with a cloth and set nearer the fire than you dared trust the dough, and let them rise for an hour. Peep under the cloth two or three times to see whether they rise evenly, and turn the pan around once that all may be equally exposed to the heat.

When the time is up and the rolls are puffy and promising, set them in a pretty quick oven and bake half an hour, turning the pan once in this time, and covering with clean—never printed—paper, should they brown too fast. Break the rolls apart from one another and eat warm. They are also good cold, and if the directions be followed implicitly, very good always.

Graham Rolls

Are made by treating the dough mixed for Graham bread as above and following the foregoing receipt in every section, but allowing more time for rising and baking. They are even better when cold than hot.

Breakfast Biscuit.

Two cups of fresh milk slightly warmed.

One quart and a cup of flour sifted.

Five tablespoonfuls of yeast.

One even tablespoonful of white sugar.

One even teaspoonful of salt.

Bit of soda as large as a pea, dissolved in hot water.

One tablespoonful of butter, just melted, not hot.

Yolk of one egg beaten light.

Sift the flour, salt and sugar into a bowl, hollow the heap in the centre and pour in the milk, working down the flour into the liquid with a spoon or your hands until it is thoroughly melted. Into a second hollow pour the yeast and knead thoroughly for fifteen minutes. Wrap bowl and biscuit in a thick cloth and set to rise where it will neither become chilled nor sour over night. (Study the temperature in different parts of the kitchen and kitchen closets to the end of finding the best places for raising dough and sponge.)

Do all this at bedtime. Early in the morning turn out the dough upon a floured board, work it for a minute into manageable shape; drill several finger-holes in it and fill them with the melted butter, the dissolved soda and the beaten yolk of egg. Pinch the dough hard to stop the mouths of these cavities, and knead for ten minutes, carefully at first, lest the liquids should be wasted, and more boldly when they are absorbed by the paste. Roll out into a sheet half an inch thick with a floured rolling-pin; cut into round cakes, set these closely together in a well-greased pan; prick each with a fork and let them rise near the fire for half an hour, covered with a light cloth.

Bake from twenty to twenty-five minutes in a quick oven, turning the pan around once, quickly and lightly. Break apart from one another and pile on a plate, throwing a clean doily or a small napkin over them. Break open at table. Hot rolls and muffins should never be cut.

One word with regard to getting up early in order to give dough a chance for the second rising. It is *not* a wholesome practice for any woman—least of all a young girl to be out of bed two hours before she eats her breakfast. Studying upon an empty stomach provokes dyspepsia and injures the eyes. Active exercise in like circumstances tempts debility and disease. Yet our bread and rolls must be looked after at the proper time. Have yourself called on biscuit mornings an hour earlier than usual. Rise, wash face and hands, rinse the mouth out and brush back the hair. Put on stockings and slippers, such underclothing as may be needed to prevent cold, a wrapper and the kitchen apron. Cover your hair entirely with a handkerchief or sweeping cap. Before beginning operations down-stairs eat a half-slice of dry bread or a biscuit. You will not relish it, but take it all the same to appease the empty, discontented stomach. Having made out your rolls and tucked them up snugly for the final rise, return to your chamber for a comfortable bath and toilet. When habited for the day in all except the outer gown, collar, etc., slip on the wrapper again and run down to put the biscuits in the oven. Unless it is *too* hot, they will get no harm while you finish dressing in ten minutes, just in season to turn the pan.

From the beginning of your apprenticeship in housewifery, learn how to "dovetail" your duties neatly into one another. A wise accommodation of parts and angles, and compactness in the adjustment of "must-be-dones" are better than mere personal strength in the accomplishment of such tasks as fall to women to perform. Master these, and do not let them master you. Weave the little duties in and under and among what seem to be the greater. While your bread is taking a three hours' rise, you are free in body and mind for other things. The grand secret of keeping house well and without worry, lies in the art of packing and fitting different kinds of work and in picking up the minutes. Other things besides rising dough get on quite as well without your standing by to watch them.

3
BREAKFAST BREADS.

UNDER this head may be classed muffins, griddle-cakes, crumpets, corn bread, Sally Lunn, quick biscuits, and a dozen other varieties of warm bread suitable for breakfast and tea. They furnish a very pleasant variety in the daily bill of fare, and are extremely popular.

Nor are they unwholesome if properly made and cooked, and eaten by well people. To weak and impaired digestive organs all kinds of warm bread are hurtful.

English Muffins.

One quart of sifted flour.

Two cups of lukewarm water.

Half a cup of yeast.

One tablespoonful of butter melted, but not hot.
One teaspoonful of salt sifted with the flour.

Sift the flour and salt into a bowl, make a hole in the middle and pour in yeast and warm water. Stir down the flour gradually into the liquid, and when all is in, beat hard with a wooden spoon. Should the mixture be too stiff for this, add a little more water. It should be about half as thick as bread-dough. Beat for five minutes and set aside to rise, with a cloth thrown over the bowl, in a moderately warm corner.

Early in the morning stir the melted butter into the dough, beat hard for two minutes, and leave for half an hour in the covered bowl in a warm place —such as on a stool near the fire—turning it several times.

Grease muffin-rings well with sweet lard, arrange them upon a greased griddle set over the fire and already warmed (not really hot), fill about half-way to the top with batter, and bake quickly. When the dough fills the rings and begins to look firm on the top, slip a knife under one and peep at the under side. If it is delicately browned, turn the rings over with a spatula or cake-turner. This must be done quickly and dexterously, so as not to spill the batter.

When quite done, wrap a thick cloth about your fingers, take up the muffin-rings one by one; pass a sharp knife around the inside of each, to loosen the muffin, and shake it out upon a hot plate. Pile them up neatly and cover with a clean napkin. These muffins must be broken, not cut open, and buttered while hot.

The English split, toast and butter cold muffins.

Crumpets.

Two cups of lukewarm milk.

Two thirds of a cup of lukewarm water.

One quart of sifted flour.

One tablespoonful of white sugar.

Half a teaspoonful of salt.

Two tablespoonfuls of melted butter.

Half a cupful of yeast.

Soda the size of a pea, dissolved in a teaspoonful of boiling water.

Mix milk, yeast, water, sugar and salted flour as directed in former receipt. Beat hard, and set to rise over night. In the morning work in the butter and soda, beat up for one whole minute until the mixture is light throughout, and half-fill greased patty-pans with it. Set these in a baking-pan, cover with a cloth, and let them stand in a warm place fifteen minutes before putting them into a steady oven. They should be done in from twelve to fifteen minutes if the oven is right. If they brown too fast, cover them with paper.

Quick Muffins.

One quart of sifted flour.

One tablespoonful of salt.

Three cups lukewarm milk.

Two eggs.

One tablespoonful of melted butter.

Two teaspoonfuls of baking powder.

Sift flour, baking-powder and salt *twice* through the sieve, to make sure these are well mixed together. Beat the eggs very light. (By all means have a Dover Egg-Beater for this purpose. It whips eggs to a lovely froth with less labor and in less time than any other yet invented.)

Stir melted butter, eggs and milk together in a large bowl, and to this add the flour, a cupful at a time, stirring very quickly and lightly down toward the middle of the bowl. Beat hard *up* one minute at the last, to break flour-lumps; half-fill greased patty-pans with the batter, and then bake in a quick oven.

Turn out and eat while puffy and hot.

Sally Lunn. (The "Genuine Article.")

One quart of sifted flour.

One cup of warm milk.

One of warm water.

Four large tablespoonfuls of yeast.

Two tablespoonfuls of melted butter.

Four eggs.

One tablespoonful of salt sifted with the flour.

Soda the size of a pea, dissolved in a teaspoonful of boiling water.

Beat the eggs steadily four minutes. Have ready in a bowl the warmed milk, water, melted butter and soda. Into this stir the salted flour, cupful by cupful, until all is in. Beat smooth from lumps and add the yeast. The eggs should now be whipped three minutes with the "Dover," in a cool bowl. They will not froth in a hot or warm one. When light, beat well into the batter, and then beat *up* hard for a full minute. A wooden spoon is best for this purpose. Butter a tin cake-mould well in every part, and put in the batter. If there is more than enough to half-fill the mould have two prepared, that the contents may not overflow in rising.

Set in a moderately warm place for six hours at least, and then bake in the mould for three quarters of an hour if there is but one loaf, half an hour if there are two.

The oven must be steady and not very hot at first. Turn the mould twice in this time keeping the oven door open as short a time as possible. When you think the loaf is done, thrust a clean straw down into the thickest part.

If it comes up as clean as when it went in, take out the bread. Slip a knife around the edge to loosen it, and turn out upside down on a warm plate.

Cut in triangular slices at table, holding the knife upright to avoid crushing and making it heavy.

Quick Biscuits.

One quart of sifted flour.

Two heaping tablespoonfuls of sweet, firm lard.

Two cups of new milk (warm from the cow if you can get it.)

Two tablespoonfuls of baking powder.

One teaspoonful of salt.

Sift salt, flour, and baking-powder twice into a bowl or tray. With a clean sharp chopping-knife work the lard into this, turning and chopping until no lumps are left. Into a hollow in the middle pour the milk, working the flour downward until you have a soft, wet mass, using the chopper for this purpose. Flour your pastry-board and your hands, make the dough into a ball, handling it as little as possible, and lay on the board. Roll out with a floured rolling-pin into a sheet half an inch in thickness, and with *very few strokes*. Cut into round cakes, sift flour lightly over the bottom of a baking-pan, and set your biscuits—just *not* touching one another—in even rows within it.

Bake about twelve minutes in a quick oven. The dough should have a rough appearance before it is baked, like what is known as "pebbled morocco." Too much handling will make it sleek without and tough within.

You can make excellent quick biscuits by the above receipt, by substituting Hecker's Prepared Flour for the barreled family flour, and omitting the baking-powder. You will, however, probably be obliged to add a little more milk, as prepared flour "thickens up" rather more than other brands.

4
OTHER BREAKFAST BREADS.

Griddle Cakes.

IN making these, let quickness be the first, second and third rules. Beat briskly and thoroughly; mix just as you are ready to send the cakes to the table (except when yeast is used), bake, turn, and serve promptly. Have all your materials on the table, measured and ready to your hand. The griddle must be perfectly clean and wiped off with a dry cloth just before you lay it on the stove. Heat it gradually at one side of the stove or range, and when it is warm grease with a bit of fat salt pork stuck firmly on a fork. The fat should be hissing hot, but not scorching, when the batter is poured on. Before putting the cakes on to fry, slip the griddle to the hottest part of the stove. Drop the batter in great, even spoonfuls, and be careful not to spill or spatter it.

M. H. Phillips and Co., of Troy, N. Y., manufacture a griddle with three shallow cups sunken in an iron plate which moves on a hinge. When the cakes are done on the lower side the turn of a handle reverses the plate upon a heated surface. This makes the cakes of equal size and thickness and saves the trouble of watching, spatula in hand, to turn each one. It greatly simplifies the process of baking cakes, and, lessens the heating labor of attending to them.

Be sure that each cake is done before you turn it. A twice-turned "griddle" is spoiled.

Sour-milk Cakes.

One quart of "loppered," or of buttermilk.

Three cups of sifted flour.

One cup of Indian meal.

One "rounded" teaspoonful of soda free from lumps.

One teaspoonful of salt.

Two tablespoonfuls of molasses.

Sift flour, salt and meal into a bowl. In another mix the milk, molasses and soda. Stir these last to a foam, and pour into the hollow in the middle of the flour. Work down the flour into the liquid with a wooden spoon until you have a batter, and beat *hard* with upward strokes, two minutes. Bake at once. These are cheap, easy and good cakes.

Hominy Cakes.

Two cups of fine hominy boiled and cold. (Take the tough skin from the top before mixing in the batter.)

One heaping cup of sifted flour.

One quart of milk.

Three eggs beaten very light.

One tablespoonful of molasses.

One teaspoonful of salt.

Rub the hominy with the back of a wooden spoon until all the lumps are broken up. Wet it little by little with the milk and molasses, working it smooth as you go on. Sift flour and salt together, and put in next. Beat for a whole minute before adding the whipped eggs, and another minute very hard, before baking. Stir up well from the bottom before putting each fresh batch of cakes on the griddle.

These cakes if properly made, are tender, wholesome and delightful.

Graham Cakes.

Two cups of Graham flour.

One of sifted white.

One heaping tablespoonful of Indian meal.

Three cups of buttermilk, or loppered milk.

One rounded teaspoonful of soda.

Two tablespoonfuls of molasses.

One teaspoonful of salt sifted with the flour.

Two eggs whipped very light.

One tablespoonful melted butter.

Put Graham and salted white flour into a bowl with the Indian meal. Stir up in another milk, molasses, soda and melted butter, and while foaming pour into the hollowed flour. Work to a good batter and beat in the eggs already whipped to a froth.

Beat one minute and bake at once.

This is a good standard breakfast hot bread.

5
EGGS.

MANY people do not know a well-boiled egg by sight or taste, yet a *fresh* egg, boiled to a nicety, is one of the simplest, most nutritious of breakfast dishes.

Boiled Eggs.

Select the cleanest eggs, wash them well, and lay them in lukewarm water for five minutes. Have ready on the fire a saucepan of water on a fast boil, and in quantity sufficient to cover the eggs entirely. Into this put one egg at a time with a spoon, depositing each gently on the bottom, and quickly.

Four minutes boils an egg thoroughly, if one likes the white set and the yolk heated to the centre. *Five minutes* makes the white firm and sets the yolk. *Ten minutes* boils both hard.

Take up the eggs with a split spoon or wire whisk. If you have no regular egg dish, lay a heated napkin in a deep dish or bowl (also warmed), put in the eggs as in a nest, cover up with the corners of the napkin, and send directly to the table. They harden in the shells if left long without being broken.

The best way to manage a boiled egg at the table is the English way of setting it upright in the small end of the egg-cup, making a hole in the top large enough to admit the egg-spoon, and eating it from the shell, seasoning as you go on. Heat and taste are undoubtedly better preserved by this method than by any other. Those who cannot afford gold-washed spoons, can procure pretty ivory ones at a trifling cost, or small teaspoons will serve the purpose.

Spoons smeared with eggs should be laid to soak in *cold* water directly you have finished using them.

Custard Eggs.

Put the washed eggs in a saucepan of cold water and let them just come to a boil, then take them up.

Or, lay them in a hot tin pail, cover them with boiling water, put the top on the pail and leave them on the kitchen table for five minutes. Drain off the water, pour on more *boiling* hot and replace the top. Wrap a hot towel about the pail, and leave it four minutes before dishing the eggs. They will be like a soft custard throughout, and more digestible than if cooked in any other way.

Poached, or Dropped Eggs.

Into a clean frying-pan, pour plenty of boiling water, and a teaspoonful of salt. Let it boil steadily, not violently. Wipe a cup dry, break an egg into it, and pour, very cautiously and quickly, on the surface of the water. Avoid spreading or breaking it. It will sink to the bottom for an instant, but if the water is boiling hot, will rise soon and be cooked in about three and a half minutes. Do not put more than three into the pan at one time, or they will run into one another.

Take them up with a perforated skimmer and lay on a hot, flat dish in which a teaspoonful of butter has been melted. If the whites have ragged edges, trim neatly with a sharp knife. When all are done, pepper and salt lightly, put a bit of butter on each egg and send up *very hot*.

Eggs on Toast.

Cut out with a sharp-edged tumbler or a cake cutter as many round slices of stale bread as there are eggs to be cooked. Toast these nicely, butter thinly; cover the bottom of a heated dish with them, and pour on each a tablespoonful of boiling water. Set in the plate-warmer or an open oven while you poach eggs as directed in the last receipt.

Lay each when done on a round of toast, pepper, salt and butter, and serve.

Eggs on Savory Toast.

Toast rounds of stale bread as directed in preceding receipt, but instead of moistening them with hot water, pour upon them, as they lie in the dish, two tablespoonfuls of boiling gravy to each slice. A half-cupful of gravy left over from yesterday's roast or stew skimmed free of fat, heated, thinned with a very little boiling water, well-seasoned, then strained and boiled up quickly, makes this a tempting dish.

Poach as many eggs as you have rounds of toast, and lay on these, with pepper, salt and bits of butter.

Scrambled or Stirred Eggs.

Nine eggs.

One tablespoonful of butter.

Half a teaspoonful of salt.

A little pepper.

Half a teaspoonful of chopped parsley very fine.

Break the eggs altogether in a bowl. Put the butter in a clean frying-pan and set it on the range. As it melts, add pepper, salt and parsley. When it hisses, pour in the eggs, and begin at once to stir them, scraping the bottom of the pan from the sides toward the centre, until you have a soft, moist mass just firm enough not to run over the bottom of the heated dish on which you turn it out. Make it into a neat mound. Some people prefer it without the parsley.

In serving *everything*, be careful that the rims of the dishes are perfectly clean. The effect of the most delicious viand is spoiled by drops or smears of food on the vessel containing it.

If you heap your scrambled eggs on a platter and lay parsley-sprigs around, making a green fringe or border for the yellow hillock, you have an elegant dish. Study to make plain things pretty when you can.

Bacon and Eggs.

Fry as many slices of ham, or what is known as breakfast-bacon, as there are eggs to be cooked. Have the clean frying-pan warm, but not hot, when the meat goes in. Turn the slices as they brown. When done, take the pan over to the sink or table, remove the meat to a hot dish and set where it will keep warm.

Strain the grease left in the pan through a bit of tarlatan or coarse muslin into a cup. Wipe the frying-pan clean, pour in the strained fat and return to the fire. If there is not enough to cover the bottom a quarter of an inch deep, add a tablespoonful of butter. Break the eggs one at a time in a cup, and when the fat hisses put them in carefully.

Few people like "turned" fried eggs. Slip a cake-turner or spatula under each as it cooks to keep it from sticking. They should be done in about three minutes. Do not put in more at once than can swim in the fat without interfering with one another.

Take up as fast as they cook, trim off ragged and rusty edges and lay on a hot platter. Drain each to get rid of the fat, as you take it out of the pan.

When all are dished, lay the ham or bacon neatly about the eggs like a garnish. Pepper all lightly. Ham for this purpose should be cut in small narrow slices.

Drop sprays of parsley on the rim of the dish.

Baked Eggs.

Put a tablespoonful of butter in a pie-plate, and set in the oven until it melts and begins to smoke. Take it to the table and break six eggs one by one into a cup, pouring each in turn into the melted butter carefully. Sprinkle with pepper and salt, put a tiny bit of butter on each and set in the oven to bake until the eggs are "set"—that is, when the whites are firm and the yolks skimmed over, but not hard. Four minutes in a quick oven should do this. Send to table at once.

If you have a few spoonfuls of nice chicken gravy, you can strain and use it instead of butter.

Scalloped Eggs.

Six eggs.

Half a cupful of nice gravy skimmed and strained. Chicken, turkey, game and veal gravy are especially good for this purpose. Clear soup may also be used.

Half a cupful of pounded cracker or fine dry bread-crumbs.

Pepper and salt.

Pour the gravy into a pie-plate and let it get warm before putting in the eggs as in last receipt. Pepper, salt and strew cracker crumbs evenly over them. Bake five minutes. Serve in the pie-plate.

Dropped Eggs with White Sauce.

Drop or poach the eggs; put them on a hot, flat dish and pour over them this sauce boiling hot.

In a saucepan put half a cupful of boiling water.

Two or three large spoonfuls of nice strained gravy.

A little pepper.

A quarter teaspoonful of salt.

When this boils stir in a heaping teaspoonful of flour wet up smoothly with a little cold water to keep it from lumping. Stir and boil one minute and add a tablespoonful of butter. Stir steadily two minutes longer, add, if you like, a little minced parsley, and pour the sauce which should be like thick cream, over the dished eggs.

Omelette.

Six eggs.

Four teaspoonfuls of cream.

Half a teaspoonful salt.

A little pepper.

Two tablespoonfuls of butter.

Whip whites and yolks together for four minutes in a bowl with the "Dover" egg beater. They should be thick and smooth before you beat in cream, salt and pepper. Melt the butter in a clean frying-pan, set on one side of the stove where it will keep warm but not scorch. Pour the beaten mixture into it and remove to a place where the fire is hotter. As it "sets," slip a broad knife carefully around the edges and under it, that the butter may find its way freely to all parts of the pan.

When the middle is just set, pass a cake-turner *carefully* under one half of the omelette and fold it over the other. Lay a hot platter upside down above the doubled mass and holding frying-pan and dish firmly, turn the latter quickly over, reversing the positions of the two, and depositing the omelette in the dish.

Do not be mortified should you break your trial omelette. Join the bits neatly; lay sprays of parsley over the cracks and try another soon. Be sure it is loosened from the pan before you try to turn it out; hold pan and dish fast in place; do not be nervous or flurried, and you will soon catch the knack of dishing the omelette dexterously and handsomely.

I have given you ten receipts for cooking eggs. It would be easy to furnish as many more without exhausting the list of ways of preparing this invaluable article of food for our tables. I have selected the methods that are at once easy and excellent, and adapted to the ability of a class of beginners.

6
BROILED MEATS.

IT has been said that the frying-pan has ruined more American digestions than all the other hurtful agencies combined. It is certainly true that while the process of frying *properly* performed upon certain substances does not of necessity, make them unwholesome—the useful utensil does play altogether too important a part in our National cookery. Broiled meats are more wholesome, more palatable, and far more elegant. Certain things should never be fried. That beefsteak should *never* make the acquaintance of the frying-pan is a rule without an exception.

The best gridirons for private families are the light, double "broilers," made of tinned wire and linked together at the back with loops of the same material. They are easily handled, turned and cleansed, and when not in use may be hung on the wall out of the way. It is well to have two sizes, one for large steaks, the smaller for birds, oysters, and when there is occasion to broil a single chop or chicken-leg for an invalid.

Beefsteak.

Never wash a steak unless it has fallen in the dirt or met with other accident. In this case cleanse quickly in cold water and wipe perfectly dry before cooking.

Have a clear hot fire and do not uncover that part of the stove above it until you have adjusted the steak on the broiler. If you use the ordinary iron gridiron, lay the meat on it the instant it goes over the fire, but have it already warm and rub the bars with a bit of fresh suet.

When the meat has lain over the coals two minutes and begins to "sizzle," turn it and let the other side cook as long. Watch it continually and turn whenever it begins to drip. Do this quickly to keep in the juices. If these should fall in the fire in spite of your care, lift it for an instant and hold over a plate or dish until the smoke is gone. Broiled meats flavored with creosote are not uncommon, but always detestable. The knack of broiling a steak well is to turn it so often and dexterously that it will neither be smoked nor scorched.

Ten minutes should cook it rare, if the fire is right and the steak not very thick. Cut with a keen blade into the thickest part when the time is up. If the heart is of a rich red-brown—not the livid purple of uncooked flesh, carry broiler and meat to a table where stands a hot dish. Lay the steak on this. In a saucer have a liberal tablespoonful of butter cut into bits, and with these rub both sides of the smoking steak, leaving unmelted pieces on the top. Sprinkle it also on both sides with pepper and salt—about half a teaspoonful of salt and a third as much pepper for a large steak. All this must be done *quickly*. Before you begin to cook the steak, prepare the butter and measure the salt and pepper. Cover the dish closely. If you have not a block-tin dish-cover, lay over the steak another dish, made very hot in the oven, and set both with the meat between them in the plate-warmer, or in an open oven, or somewhere where it will keep hot for three minutes.

Serve—i. e. put on the table—as hot as possible and on warm plates. Unless you have a hot water dish, do not send the steak into the dining-room until all have taken their places.

Sometimes steak is tough. You shake your head over it as it comes from the butcher's basket. I know of an enterprising meat merchant who objected to a wealthy customer because he would have choice cuts. He was willing to pay double for them, but as the worthy seller observed: "We *must* sell second-best cuts, and he'd ought to take his turn."

Like sin, tough steak ought not to be, but it *is!* If your turn to take it has come, lay it on a clean board, some hours before cooking it, and hack it on both sides, criss-cross, with a tolerably sharp knife, taking care not to cut too deeply. Rub both sides very well with the strained juice of a lemon, and set the meat in a cold place until you are ready to cook it. Do this over night, if you want it for breakfast. Very tough, fibrous meat is sometimes made eatable by this process.

Mutton or Lamb Chops.

Cut off most of the fat and all the skin. A clean bone an inch in length will project from the smaller end when you have pared away the tallow and skin which would have cooked into rankness and leather.

Put as many chops on the broiler as it will conveniently hold, and broil as you would beefsteak. Cut into the largest to see if it is done. If it is, lay the chops on a heated dish set over a pot of boiling water; butter, pepper and salt them, and cover them up while you cook the rest.

Serve as soon as the last is cooked, as they lose flavor with standing.

Lay sprigs of parsley around the edges of the dish and scatter a few over the chops which must be arranged in neat rows, a small end next to a large.

Broiled Ham.

Cut even slices from a cold boiled Ferris & Co.'s "Trade Mark" ham. Divide these into oblong pieces about an inch and a half in width, and broil quickly over clear coals until a delicate brown touches the slices here and there. Lay in order on a hot dish. Broiled ham is appetizing, and should be accompanied by dry toast, lightly buttered.

7
FRIED MEATS.

Larded Liver.

THE butcher will slice the liver, or show you how to do it. When it is cut up, lay it in cold water in which has been stirred a teaspoonful of salt. This will draw out the blood.

Cut fat, raw salt pork into strips a finger long and a quarter of an inch thick and wide.

In half an hour's time take the liver from the water, spread it out on a clean dry cloth, lay another cloth over the slices and pat gently to dry them thoroughly. Make holes an inch apart in the liver with a pen-knife or sharp skewer, and stick in the pork strips. They should protrude an equal distance on both sides.

As fast as they are ready, lay them in a clean, warm (*not* hot) frying-pan. When all are in, set it over the fire, and let it fry rather slowly in the fat that will run out from the pork "lardoons." In five minutes turn the slices, and again ten minutes later. Let the liver heat quite slowly for the first ten minutes. If cooked fast it is hard and indigestible. Allow about twenty-five minutes for frying it.

Take it up with a fork, draining off every drop of grease against the side of the pan as you remove each piece, and dish on a hot platter.

Put a half a teaspoonful of tomato sauce on each slice. Serve without gravy and very hot.

Veal Cutlets (Breaded).

Whip two eggs light and pour them into a pie-plate. Turn the cutlets, one by one, over in this until every part is coated. In another dish spread evenly a cupful of rolled or pounded cracker, very fine and dry. Turn the "egged" cutlets over in this to encrust them well.

Meanwhile four large spoonfuls of sweet lard or nice beef-dripping must be melting in a clean frying-pan at one side of the range. When the cutlets are all breaded, move the pan directly over the fire. As the fat begins a lively hiss, put in as many cutlets as can lie in it without crowding. In five minutes turn them with care, not to loosen the crumb-coating. After another five minutes of rapid frying, pull the pan to a spot where the cooking will go on slowly, but regularly. In ten minutes turn the cutlets a second time. In another ten minutes they should be done.

Understand! The first fast cooking sears the surface of the meat and forms the breading into a firm crust that keeps in the juices. The slower work that follows cooks the veal thoroughly without hardening the fibres.

Lift the cutlets carefully from the pan, draining all the grease from each, and keep hot in a covered dish set over a pot of boiling water until all are done.

Always put tomato catsup or tomato sauce, in some form, on the table with veal cutlets.

Sausage Cakes.

Break off bits of sausage meat of equal size, roll them in the palms of clean hands into balls and pat them into flat cakes. Arrange them in a frying-pan and cook (not too fast) in their own fat, turning them twice until they are nicely and evenly browned. The time allowed for frying them depends on the size of the cakes. If they are not large, fifteen minutes should be enough.

Serve on a hot dish, without gravy.

Smothered Sausages.

Prick "link" sausages—that is, those done up in skins, in fifteen or twenty places, with a large needle; put them in a clean frying-pan in which is a half a teacup full of hot water. Roll the sausages over in this several times and cover *closely*. If you have not the lid of a pot or of a tin-pail that fits the frying-pan, use a pie-dish turned upside down. Set the pan where the water will bubble slowly, for ten minutes. Lift the cover then, and roll the sausages over again two or three times, to wet them thoroughly, leaving them with the sides up that were down. Cover again and cook ten minutes longer. Turn them twice more, at intervals of five minutes, cover, and let them steam four minutes before taking them up. They will be plump, whole, tender and well-done, and the bottom of the pan be almost dry. Lay in neat rows on a hot dish.

Fish Balls.

Soak a pound of cod-fish all night in cold water. Change it in the morning, and cover with lukewarm water for three hours more. Wash it, scraping off the salt and fat; put it into a sauce-pan, cover it well with water just blood-warm, and let it simmer—that is, not *quite* boil, two hours. Take it up, pick out the bones and remove the skin, and set the fish aside to cool.

When perfectly cold chop it fine in a wooden tray. Have ready, for a cupful of minced fish, nearly two cupfuls of potato boiled and mashed very smooth.

> A tablespoonful of butter.
>
> Half a teaspoonful of salt.
>
> Two tablespoonfuls of milk worked into the fish while hot.
>
> Add also, when the potato has been rubbed until free from lumps, the beaten yolk of an egg. Work this in well with a wooden or silver spoon.
>
> Now stir in the chopped fish, a little at a time, mixing all together until you have a soft mass which you can handle easily.

Drop a tablespoonful of the mixture on a floured pastry board, or a floured dish. Flour your hands, roll the fish and potato into a ball, and pat it into a cake, or make it as round as a marble. Lay these as you form them on a dish dusted with flour, and when all are made out, set in a cool place until morning.

Half an hour before breakfast, have five or six great spoonfuls of sweet lard hissing hot in a frying-pan or doughnut-kettle. Put in the balls a few at a time; turn as they color; take them out when they are of a tanny brown, lay them in a hot colander set in a plate, and keep warm in the open oven until all are fried.

A Breakfast Stew (very nice).

> Two pounds of lean beef. (The "second best cuts" may be used here.)
>
> A quarter of a medium-sized onion.
>
> A tablespoonful of browned flour.
>
> Half a teaspoonful each of minced parsley, summer savory, and sweet marjoram.
>
> As much allspice as will lie on a silver dime.
>
> One teaspoonful of Halford sauce.
>
> One saltspoonful of made mustard.
>
> One saltspoonful of pepper.
>
> Strained juice of half a lemon.

Cut the meat into pieces an inch square. Put it with the chopped onion into a saucepan with a pint of lukewarm water; cover closely and cook slowly, *at least* two hours and a half. The meat should not be allowed to boil hard at any time, and when done, be so tender that it is ready to fall to pieces.

Pour the stew into a bowl, add the salt and pepper, cover it and set in a cool place until next morning.

Then put it back into the sauce-pan, set it over a quick fire, and when it begins to boil, stir in the spice and herbs. (The latter may be bought dried and powdered at the druggist's if you cannot get them fresh.)

Boil up sharply five minutes.

The flour should be browned the day before, by spreading it on a tin plate and setting this on the stove, stirring constantly to keep it from burning black. Or a better way is, to set the tin plate in a hot oven, opening the door now and then to stir it. It is a good plan to brown a good deal—say a cupful of flour—at a time, and keep it in a glass jar for thickening gravies, etc.

Wet up a heaping tablespoonful of this with three tablespoonfuls of cold water, the lemon-juice, mustard and Worcestershire sauce. Rub smooth and stir well into the stew. Boil two minutes longer to thicken the gravy and turn out into a deep covered dish.

This is a good dinner, as well as breakfast dish. A teaspoonful of catsup is an improvement.

8
WHAT TO DO WITH "LEFT-OVERS."

A VOLUME, instead of a single chapter, might be written upon the various methods of preparing what the French call "*rechauffés,*" and we speak of, usually contemptuously, as "warmed-over" meats. Cold meat is seldom tempting except to the very hungry. Cold tongue, ham and poultry are well enough on picnics and as a side-dish at tea. At breakfast they are barely admissible; for a simple luncheon tolerable; for dinner hardly excusable. At the first and last meal of the day, the stomach craves something hot and relishable.

A wife told me, once, with strong disgust in the remembrance, that when her husband took her on the wedding-trip to visit his mother, a frugal Massachusetts matron, they were set down within half an hour after their arrival, to lunch on a cold eel-pie left from the day before. The daughter-in-law, forty years later, spoke feelingly of the impression of niggardliness and inhospitality made on her mind by the incident.

"If she had even warmed it up, I should not have felt so forlornly homesick," she said. "But cold eel-pie! Think of it!"

I confess to heartfelt sympathy with the complainant. There is a suggestion of friendliness and home-comfort in the "goodly smell" of a steaming-hot *entrée* set before family or guest. It argues forethought for those who are to be fed. We have the consciousness that we are expected and that somebody has cared enough for us to make ready a visible welcome. Pale slices of cold mutton, and thin slabs of corned beef cannot, with the best intentions on the part of the caterer, convey this.

The summing up of this lecture, is: Neither despise unlikely fragments left over from roast, baked or boiled, nor consider them good enough as they are without "rehabilitation."

We will begin with a dish the mention of which provokes a sneer more often than any other known to civilization.

Hash.

Rid cold corned or roast beef of fat, skin and gristle, and mince it in a wooden tray with a sharp chopper until the largest piece is not more than an eighth of an inch square.

With two cupfuls of this mix a cupful of mashed potato rubbed smooth with a potato beater or wooden spoon.

Season well with pepper and salt if the beef be fresh, if corned use the salt sparingly and pepper well.

Set a clean frying-pan on the stove with a cupful of beef gravy in it from which you have skimmed all the fat. Clear soup will do if you have no gravy. If you have neither, pour into the pan a half-pint of boiling water and stir into this three tablespoonfuls of butter. When the butter-water (or gravy) reaches the boil, add a half-teaspoonful of made mustard.

Then put in the meat and potato and stir—scraping the bottom of the pan to prevent sticking—for five minutes, or until you have a bubbling-hot mass, not stiff, nor yet semi-liquid. It must have been brought to boiling heat and kept at it about five minutes, cooking so fast that you have to stir and toss constantly lest it should scorch.

Heap on a hot dish, and eat from hot plates.

Hash Cakes.

Having prepared the hash as above set it aside until cold, when mould into flat cakes as you would sausage meat, and roll in flour. Heat nice beef-dripping to a boil in a frying-pan, lay in the cakes, and fry to a light brown on both sides.

Beef Croquettes.

You can make these of the cold hash by moulding it into rolls about three and a half inches long, and rather more than an inch in diameter. Roll these over and over on a floured dish or board to get them smooth and regular in shape; flatten the ends by setting each upright on the floury dish, and put enough dripping in the pan to cover them as they lie on their sides in it. It should be *very* hot before they go in.

Roll over carefully in the fat as they brown, not to spoil the shape. Do not put too many in the pan at once; as fast as they are done take them up and lay in a hot colander until all are ready. Arrange neatly on a heated flat dish and serve.

A Mutton Stew.

Cut slices of cold mutton half an inch thick, trim away fat and skin and divide the lean meat into neat squares about an inch across.

Drop a piece of onion as large as a hickory-nut in a cupful of water and boil fifteen minutes. Strain the water through a bit of muslin, squeezing the onion hard to extract the flavor. Allow this cupful of water to two cupfuls of meat. If you have less mutton use less water; if more increase the quantity of liquid.

Pour the water into a clean saucepan and when it boils add two full tablespoonfuls of butter cut into bits and rolled over and over in browned flour until no more will adhere to the butter.

Stir this in with a little pepper and salt, a pinch of mace and a teaspoonful of lemon-juice. Boil up once and drop in the meat. Cover closely and let it simmer at one side of the stove, almost, but never *quite* boiling, for ten minutes.

Turn into a deep dish and serve very hot.

Minced Mutton on Toast.

Trim off skin and fat from slices of cold mutton and mince in a chopping-tray. Season with pepper and salt.

Into a clean frying-pan, pour a cupful of mutton-gravy which has been skimmed well, mixed with a little hot water and strained through a bit of coarse muslin.

When this boils, wet a teaspoonful of browned flour with three tablespoonfuls of cold water, and a teaspoonful of tomato or walnut catsup, or half a teaspoonful of Worcestershire sauce. Rub out all the lumps and stir into the gravy in the frying-pan. Boil up once well before putting in the mutton.

As soon as the mixture bubbles and smokes all over, draw it to one side of the range where it will keep hot, but not quite boil; cover it closely, and let it stand five minutes. Warmed-over mutton becomes insipid when cooked too much.

Before the mince is put into the pan, toast the bread. Cut thick slices from a stale loaf, and trim off the crust. If you would have them look particularly nice, cut them round with a cake or biscuit-cutter. Toast to a light-brown, and keep hot until the mince is cooked.

Then lay the toast on a heated platter; butter the rounds well on both sides, and pour on each a tablespoonful of *boiling* water. Heap a great spoonful of the minced mutton on each piece.

The mince should not be a stiff paste, nor yet so soft as to run all over the dish. A cupful of gravy will be enough for three cupfuls of meat.

Some people fancy a little green pickle or chow chow chopped very fine and mixed in with the mince while cooking. Others think the dish improved by the addition of a teaspoonful of lemon-juice put in just before taking it from the fire.

Devilled Mutton.

Cut even slices of cold mutton, not too fat.

Stir together and melt in a clean frying-pan two tablespoonfuls of butter and one of currant or grape jelly.

When it hisses lay in the mutton and heat slowly —turning several times—for five minutes, or until the slices are soft and very hot, but not until they begin to crisp.

Take out the meat, lay on a warmed dish, cover and set over boiling water.

To the butter and jelly left in the pan add three tablespoonfuls of vinegar.

A small teaspoonful of made mustard.

A quarter spoonful of salt.

Half as much pepper as you have salt.

Stir together over the fire until they boil, and pour on the meat. Cover three minutes over boiling water, and serve.

Devilled, or Barbecued Ham.

Slice cold Ferris & Co.'s "Trade Mark" ham, lean and fat together, and lay in a clean frying-pan. Fry gently in the grease that runs from it as it heats, until the lean is soft, the fat clear and beginning to crisp at the edges.

Take out the slices with a fork, lay on a warmed dish; keep hot over boiling water.

Add to the fat left in the frying-pan:

Four tablespoonfuls of vinegar.

A small teaspoonful of made mustard.

As much pepper as will lie *easily* on a silver half-dime.

Stir until it boils, then pour on the ham. Let it stand covered over the boiling water for five minutes before sending to the table.

Chicken Croquettes.

One cup of cold chicken, minced fine.

One quarter cup of pounded cracker.

One teaspoonful of cornstarch, wet up in a *little* cold water.

One egg.

One tablespoonful of butter.

Half a tablespoonful of salt.

A good pinch of pepper.

Half a cupful of boiling water.

Mix minced chicken and crumbs together in a bowl with salt and pepper.

Put the boiling water in a clean saucepan, add the butter and set over the fire. When the butter is melted stir in the wet corn starch. Boil and stir until it thickens.

Have the egg beaten light in a bowl and pour the hot mixture upon it. Beat well, and mix with the minced chicken. Let it get perfectly cold and make into croquettes as directed for beef croquettes.

But roll these in a well-beaten egg, then in fine cracker-crumbs instead of flour, and fry, a few at a time, in a mixture half-butter, half-lard enough to cover them well. Drain off every drop of fat from each croquette as you take it up, and keep hot until all are done.

Serve hot and at once.

9
DINNER DISHES.

I AM amused and yet made thoughtful by the fact that so many young housekeepers write to me of their pleasure in cake-making and their desire to learn how to compound what are usually known as "fancy-dishes," some sending excellent receipts for loaf-cake, cookies and doughnuts, while few express the least interest in soups, meats and vegetables. The drift of the dear creatures' thoughts reminds me of a rhymed—"If I had!" which I read years ago, setting forth how a little boy would have if he could, a house built of pastry, floored with taffy, ceiled with sugar-plums, and roofed with frosted gingerbread. In engaging a cook one does not ask, first of all, "Can you get up handsome desserts?" but, "Do you understand bread-making and baking, and the management of meats, soups, and other branches of plain cookery?"

The same "plain cookery" is the pivot on which the family health and comfort rest and turn. If you would qualify yourselves to become thorough housewives, it is as essential that you should master the principles of this, as that a musician should be able to read the notes on the staff. Some people do play tolerably by ear, but they are never ranked as students, much less as professors of music. "Fancy" cookery is to the real thing what embroidery is to the art of the seamstress. She who has learned how to use her needle deftly upon "seam, gusset and band," will find the acquisition of ornamental stitches an easy matter. Skill in Kensington and satin stitch is of little value in fitting one to do "fine," which is also useful sewing.

I am sorry to add that my observation goes to prove that more American housekeepers can make delicate and rich cake than excellent soups.

Soup Stock.

Two pounds coarse lean beef, chopped almost as
fine as sausage-meat.

One pound of lean veal—also chopped.

Two pounds of bones (beef, veal, or mutton) cracked in several places.

Half an onion chopped.

Two or three stalks of celery, when you can get it.

Five quarts of cold water.

Meat and bones should be raw, but if you have bones left from underdone beef or mutton, you may crack and add them. Put all the ingredients (no salt or pepper) in a large clean pot, cover it closely and set at one side of the range where it will not get really hot under two hours. This gives the water time to draw out the juices of the meat. Then remove to a warmer place, stir up well from the bottom, and cook slowly five hours longer.

It should never boil hard, but "bubble-bubble" softly and steadily all the while. Fast boiling toughens the fibres and keeps in the juice of the meat which should form the body of the soup. When the time is up, lift the pot from the fire, throw in a heaping tablespoonful of salt, and a teaspoonful of pepper, and pour out into your "stock-pot." This should be a stout stone crock or jar, with a cover, and be used for nothing else.

See that it is free from grease, dust and all smell, scald out with hot water and soda, then with clean boiling water just before pouring in the soup, or the hot liquid may crack it.

Put on the cover and set in a cold place until next day.

Then take off every particle of the caked fat from the top. You can use this as dripping for frying. Soup that has globules of grease floating on the surface is unwholesome and slovenly.

Strain the skimmed liquid through a colander, squeezing the meat hard to extract every drop of nutriment. Throw away the tasteless fibres and bones when you have wrung them dry.

This process should give you about three quarts of strong "stock."

Rinse your jar well and pour back the strained stock into it to be used as the foundation of several days' soups. Season it highly and keep in a cold place—in warm weather on the ice.

I hope you will not fail to set up a "stock-pot." Every family should have one. It makes the matter of really good soups simple and easy.

Clear Soup with Sago or Tapioca.

Soak half a cup of German sago or pearl tapioca four hours in a large cup of cold water. An hour before dinner put a quart of your soup-stock on the stove and bring quickly almost to a boil. When it is hot, stir in the raw white and the shell of an egg, and, stirring frequently to prevent the egg from catching on the bottom of the pot, boil fast ten minutes.

Take off and strain through a clean thick cloth, wrung out in hot water and laid like a lining in your colander. Do not squeeze the cloth, or you will muddy the soup.

Return the liquid, when strained, to the saucepan, which must be perfectly clean; stir in the soaked tapioca and a teaspoonful of minced parsley, and simmer half an hour on the side of the range.

If necessary, add a little more seasoning.

When you have made nice clear soup once, you may, if you like, color the second supply with a little "caramel-water."

This is made by putting a tablespoonful of sugar in a tin cup and setting it over the fire until it breaks up into brown bubbles, then pouring a few tablespoonfuls of boiling water on it and stirring it until dissolved. A tablespoonful of this in a quart of clear soup will give a fine amber color and not injure the flavor. Send all soups in to table very hot.

Julienne Soup.

One quarter of a firm white cabbage, shred as for cold slaw.

One small turnip, peeled and cut into thin dice.

One carrot, peeled and cut into strips like inch-long straws.

One teaspoonful of onion shred fine.

Three raw tomatoes, peeled and cut into bits.

One tablespoonful of minced parsley, and, if you can get it, three stalks of celery cut into thin slices.

Use a sharp knife for this work and bruise the vegetables as little as possible.

When all are prepared, put them in hot water enough to cover them, throw in a teaspoonful of salt and cook gently half an hour.

Clear a quart of soup-stock as directed in the last receipt, and color it with a teaspoonful of Halford sauce, or walnut catsup.

When the vegetables are tender, turn them into a colander to drain, taking care not to mash or break them. Throw away the water in which they were boiled, and add the vegetables to the clear hot soup.

Taste, to determine if it needs more pepper or salt, and simmer all together gently twenty minutes before turning into the tureen.

White Chicken Soup (Delicious).

A tough fowl can be converted into very delicious dishes by boiling it first for soup and mincing it, when cold, for croquettes.

In boiling it, allow a quart of cold water for each pound of chicken, and set it where it will heat very slowly.

If the fowl be quite old do not let it reach a boil under two hours, then boil *very* gently four hours longer.

Throw in a tablespoonful of salt when you take it from the fire, turn chicken and liquor into a bowl and set in a cold place all night.

Next day skim off the fat, strain the broth from the chicken, shaking the colander to do this well, and put aside the meat for croquettes or a scallop.

Set three pints of the broth over the fire with a teaspoonful of chopped onion, season with salt and pepper, and let it boil half an hour. Line a colander with a thick cloth, and strain the liquid, squeezing the cloth to get the flavor of the onion.

Return the strained soup to the saucepan, with a tablespoonful of minced parsley, and bring to a boil. Meanwhile, scald in a farina kettle a cupful of milk, dropping into it a bit of soda the size of a pea.

Stir into this when hot, a tablespoonful of cornstarch wet up with cold milk. When it thickens scrape it out into a bowl in which you have two eggs whipped light. Beat all together well, and stir in, spoonful by spoonful, a cupful of the boiling soup.

Draw the soup pot to one side of the range, stir in the contents of the bowl, and let it stand—but not boil—three minutes before pouring into the tureen.

Chicken and Rice Soup

Is made as white chicken soup, but with the addition of four tablespoonfuls of rice, boiled soft, and added to the chicken liquor at the same time with the parsley. Then proceed as directed, with milk, eggs, etc.

Tomato Soup.

Add a quart of raw tomatoes, peeled and sliced, or a can of stewed tomatoes, and half a small onion to a quart of stock, and stew slowly one hour.

Strain and rub through a colander and set again over the fire.

Stir in a tablespoonful of butter cut up and rubbed into a tablespoonful of flour.

A tablespoonful of cornstarch wet up with cold water.

Season to taste with pepper and salt, boil once more and pour out.

Bean Soup.

Soak one pint of dried beans all night in lukewarm water. In the morning add three quarts of cold water, half a pound of nice salt pork, cut into strips, half an onion chopped, and three stalks of celery, cut small. Set at one side of the fire until it is very hot, then where it will cook slowly, and let it boil four hours. Stir up often from the bottom, as bean-soup is apt to scorch.

An hour before dinner, set a colander over another pot and rub the bean porridge through the holes with a stout wooden spoon, leaving the skins in the colander.

Return the soup to the fire, stir in a tablespoonful of butter rubbed in a tablespoonful of flour, and simmer gently fifteen minutes longer.

Have ready in the tureen a double handful of strips or squares of stale bread, fried like doughnuts in dripping, and drained dry. Also, half a lemon, peeled and sliced very thin.

Pour the soup on these and serve.

A Soup Maigre (without Meat).

Twelve mealy potatoes, peeled and sliced.

One quart of tomatoes—canned or fresh.

One half of an onion.

Two stalks of celery.

One tablespoonful of minced parsley.

Four tablespoonfuls of butter, cut up and rolled in flour.

One tablespoonful of cornstarch wet and dissolved in cold water.

One lump of white sugar.

Three quarts of cold water will be needed.

Parboil the sliced potatoes fifteen minutes in enough hot water to cover them well. Drain this off and throw it away. Put potatoes, tomatoes, onion, celery and parsley on in three quarts of cold water, and cook gently two hours.

Then rub them all through a colander, return the soup to the pot, drop in the sugar, season to taste with pepper and salt, boil up once and take off the scum before adding the floured butter, and when this is dissolved, the cornstarch.

Stir two minutes over the fire, and your soup is ready for the table. Very good it will prove, too, if the directions be exactly followed.

When celery is out of season, you can use instead of it, a little essence of celery, or, what is better, celery salt.

10
MEATS.

ONE of the most comico-pathetico true stories I know is that of a boy, the youngest of a large family, who, having always sat at the second table, knew nothing experimentally of the choicer portions of chicken or turkey. Being invited out to dinner as the guest of a playmate, he was asked, first of all present, "what part of the turkey he preferred."

"The *carker*" (carcass), "and a little of the *stuff*" (stuffing), "if you please," replied the poor little fellow, with prompt politeness.

It was his usual ration, and in his ignorance, he craved nothing better.

The pupil in cookery who enjoys tossing up *entrées*, and devising dainty *rechauffés*, but cannot support the thought of handling raw chickens and big-boned joints of butcher's meat, is hardly wiser than he.

It is a common fallacy to believe that this branch of the culinary art is uninteresting drudgery, fit only for the hands of the very plain hired cook.

Another mistake, almost as prevalent, lies in supposing that she can, of course, perform the duty properly. There is room for intelligent skill in so simple a process as roasting a piece of meat, nor is the task severe or repulsive. Practically, it is far more important to know how to do this well, than to be proficient in cake, jelly, and pudding making.

Roast Beef.

Have a steady, moderate fire in the stove-grate. Increase the heat when the meat is thoroughly warmed.

Lay the beef, skin side uppermost, in a clean baking-pan, and dash all over it two cups of *boiling* water in which a teaspoonful of salt has been dissolved. This sears the surface slightly, and keeps in the juices.

Shut the oven door, and do not open again for twenty minutes. Then, with a ladle or iron spoon dip up the salted water and pour it over the top of the meat, wetting every part again and again. Eight or ten ladlefuls should be used in this "basting," which should be repeated every fifteen minutes for the next hour. Allow twelve minutes to each pound of meat in roasting beef.

Do not swing the oven door wide while you baste, but slip your hand (protected by an old glove or a napkin) into the space left by the half-open door, and when you have wet the surface of the roast quickly and well, shut it up again to heat and steam.

A little care in this respect will add much to the flavor and tenderness of the beef.

Should one side of it, or the back, brown more rapidly than the rest, turn the pan in the oven, and should the water dry up to a few spoonfuls, pour in another cupful from the tea-kettle.

About twenty minutes before the time for the roasting is up, draw the pan to the oven-door, and sift flour over the meat from a flour dredger or a small sieve. Shut the door until the flour browns, then baste abundantly, and dredge again.

In five minutes, or when this dredging is brown, rub the top of the meat with a good teaspoonful of butter, dredge quickly and close the door.

If the fire is good, in a few minutes a nice brown froth will encrust the surface of the cooked meat. Lift the pan to the side table, take up the beef by slipping a strong cake-turner or broad knife under it, holding it firmly with a fork, and transfer to a heated platter.

Set in the plate-warmer, or over boiling water, while you make the gravy.

Gravy (brown).

Set the pan in which the meat was roasted, *on* the range when the beef has been removed to a dish. Scrape toward the centre the browned flour from sides and bottom and dust in a little more from your dredger as you stir. If the water has boiled away until the bottom of the pan is exposed, add a little, *boiling hot,* directly from the teakettle and stir until the gravy is of the consistency of rich cream.

Pepper to taste and pour into a gravy boat.

While I give these directions, I may remark that few people of nice taste like *made* thickened gravy with roast beef. Many prefer, instead, the red essence which follows the carver's knife and settles in the dish. The carver should give each person helped his or her choice in this matter.

I am thus explicit with regard to roasting beef because the process is substantially the same with all meats. Dash scalding water over the piece put down for cooking in this way: heat rather slowly at first, increasing the heat as you go on; baste faithfully; keep the oven open as little as may be and dredge, then baste, alternately, for twenty minutes, or so, before dishing the meat.

Roast Mutton.

Cook exactly as you would beef: but if you wish a made gravy, pour it first from the baking-pan into a bowl and set in cold water five minutes, or until the fat has risen to the top.

Skim off all of this that you can remove without disturbing the dregs. It is "mutton-tallow"—very good for chapped hands, but not for human stomachs. Return the gravy to the fire, thicken, add boiling water, if needed, and stir until smooth.

Always send currant, or grape jelly, around with mutton and lamb.

Roast Lamb.

Cook two minutes less in the pound than you would mutton. Instead of gravy, you can send in with it, if you choose

Mint Sauce.

To two tablespoonfuls of chopped mint, add a tablespoonful of white sugar and nearly two thirds of a cup of vinegar. Let them stand together ten minutes in a cool place before sending to table.

Roast Veal

Must be cooked twice as long as beef or mutton, and very well basted, the flesh being fibrous and dry. To the made gravy add two teaspoonfuls of stewed and strained tomato, or one tablespoonful of tomato catsup, and cook one minute before pouring into the gravy-boat.

Roast Turkey, Chicken or Duck.

It would not be possible for me to write such directions as would enable you to prepare a fowl for cooking. Yet I advise you to learn how to draw and dress poultry. Watch the process closely, if you have opportunity, or else ask some experienced friend to instruct you.

For the present we will suppose that our fowl is ready for the roasting pan. Lay it in tenderly, breast uppermost, pour a bountiful cup of boiling water, slightly salted, over it, if it be a chicken or duck, two cupfuls, if a turkey, and roast, basting often, about twelve minutes for each pound. When the breastbone browns, turn the fowl on one side, and as this colors, on the other, that all may be done evenly. Dredge once with flour fifteen minutes before taking up the roast and when this browns, rub all over with a tablespoonful of butter. Shut up ten minutes longer and it is ready for dishing.

Chop the liver and soft parts of the gizzard—which have been roasted with the fowl—fine, and stir into the gravy while you are making it.

Fricasseed Chicken.

Cut up a full-grown fowl into joints, dividing the back and breast into two pieces each. Lay these in cold water, slightly salted, for half an hour. Wipe dry with a clean cloth. In the bottom of a pot scatter a handful of chopped fat salt pork, with half a teaspoonful of minced onion. On this lay the pieces of chicken. Sprinkle a double handful of pork on the top with another half teaspoonful of onion, pour in carefully, enough cold water to cover all, fit on a close top, and set the pot where it will heat slowly. It should not boil under one hour at least. Increase the heat, then, but keep at a *very* gentle boil for another hour, or until the chicken is tender. The time needed for cooking will depend on the age of the fowl. Fast stewing will harden and toughen it.

When done, take out the chicken with a fork and arrange on a warm dish, covering and keeping it hot in the plate warmer or over boiling water. Add to the gravy left in the pot two tablespoonfuls of chopped parsley, a heaping tablespoonful of butter cut up in the same quantity of flour, half a teaspoonful of salt, and a quarter of a teaspoonful of pepper. Stir to a boil. Meanwhile, beat up an egg in a bowl, add a teaspoonful of cornstarch, and a small cupful of milk, and when these are mixed, a cupful of the boiling gravy. Beat hard and pour into the pot where is the rest of the gravy. Bring to a quick boil, take *at once* from the fire and pour over the chicken. Cover and let it stand over hot water three minutes before sending to table.

Smothered Chicken.

The chicken must be split down the back as for broiling, washed well and wiped dry. Lay it, breast upward, in a baking pan; pour in two cups of boiling water, in which has been dissolved a heaping tablespoonful of butter, and cover with another pan turned upside down and fitting exactly the edges of the lower one. Cook slowly half an hour, lift the cover and baste plentifully with the butter water in the pan; cover again and leave for twenty minutes more. Baste again, and yet once more in another quarter of an hour. Try the chicken with a fork to see if it is done.

An hour and ten minutes should be enough for a young fowl. Baste the last time with a tablespoonful of butter; cover and leave in the oven ten minutes longer before transferring to a hot dish. It should be of a fine yellow brown all over, but crisped nowhere.

Thicken the gravy with a tablespoonful of browned flour, wet up in a little water, salt and pepper to taste, boil up once and pour a cupful over the chicken, the rest into a gravy boat.

There is no more delightful preparation of chicken than this.

Boiled Corn Beef.

Lay in clean cold water for five or six hours when you have washed off all the salt. Wipe and put it into a pot and cover deep in cold water. Boil *gently* twenty-five minutes per pound. When done, take the pot from the fire and set in the sink with the meat in it, while you make the sauce.

Strain a large cupful of the liquor into a saucepan and set it over the fire. Wet a tablespoonful of flour up with cold water, and when the liquor boils, stir it in with a great spoonful of butter. Beat it smooth before adding the juice of a lemon. Serve in a gravy-dish. Take up the beef, letting all the liquor drain from it, and send in on a hot platter.

(Save the pot-liquor for bean soup.)

Boiled Mutton.

Sew up the leg of mutton in a stout piece of mosquito net or of "cheese cloth;" lay it in a pot and cover several inches deep with boiling water. Throw in a tablespoonful of salt, and cook twelve minutes to the pound. Take up the cloth with the meat in it and dip in *very* cold water. Remove the bag and dish the meat.

Before taking up the mutton, make your sauce, using as a base a cupful of the liquor dipped from the pot. Proceed with this as you did with the drawn butter sauce for the corned beef, but instead of the lemon juice, add two tablespoonfuls of capers if you have them. If not, the same quantity of chopped green pickle.

11
VEGETABLES.

IN attempting to make out under the above heading, a list of receipts, I have laid down my pen several times in sheer discouragement. The number and variety of esculents supplied by the American market-gardener would need for a just mention of each, a treatise several times larger than our volume. I have, therefore, selected a few of the vegetables in general use on our tables, and given the simplest and most approved methods of preparing them.

As a preface I transcribe from "Common Sense in the Household" "RULES APPLICABLE TO THE COOKING OF ALL VEGETABLES."

Have them as fresh as possible.

Pick over, wash well, and cut out all decayed parts.

Lay them when peeled in *cold* water before cooking.

If you boil them put a little salt in the water.

Cook steadily after you put them on.

Be sure they are thoroughly done.

Drain well.

Serve hot!

Potatoes (boiled).

Pare them thin with a sharp knife. The starch or meal lies, in greatest quantities, nearest to the skin. Lay in clean cold water for one hour, if the potatoes are newly gathered. Old potatoes should be left in the water for several hours. If very old, they will be the better for soaking all night. New potatoes require half an hour for boiling, and the skins are rubbed off with a coarse cloth before they are cooked. Those stored for winter use should be boiled forty-five minutes.

Wipe each dry before dropping them into a kettle of boiling water, in which has been mixed a heaping tablespoonful of salt.

Boil steadily until a fork will go easily into the largest.

Turn off the water by tipping the pot over on its side in the sink, holding the top on with a thick cloth wrapped about your hand, and leaving room at the lowest edge of the cover for the water to escape, but not for a potato to slip through.

Set the pot uncovered on the range; sprinkle a tablespoonful of salt over the potatoes, shaking the pot as you do this, and leave it where they will dry off, but not scorch, for five minutes.

Mashed Potatoes.

Boil as directed in last receipt, and when the potatoes have been dried off, remove the pot to the sink, or table, break and whip them into powder with a four-tined fork, or a split spoon. When fine, add a great spoonful of butter, whipped in thoroughly, salting to taste as you go on.

Have ready a cup of milk *almost* boiling, and beat in until the potato is soft and smooth.

Heap in a deep dish for the table.

Onions (boiled).

Remove the outer layers until you reach the sleek, silvery, crisp skins. Cook in plenty of boiling, salted water, until tender. Forty minutes should be sufficient, unless the onions are very old and large. Turn off all the water; add a cupful from the tea-kettle with one of warm milk and stew gently ten minutes.

Heat, meanwhile, in a saucepan, half a cupful of milk with a large tablespoonful of butter.

Drain the onions in a hot *clean* colander, turn them into a heated deep dish, salt and pepper lightly, and pour the boiling milk and butter over them.

Onions cooked thus are not nearly so rank of flavor as when boiled in but one water.

Tomatoes (stewed).

Put ripe tomatoes into a pan, pour boiling water directly from the kettle, upon them, and cover closely for five minutes. The skins will then come off easily.

When all are peeled, cut them up, throwing away the unripe parts and the cores, and put them into a clean saucepan with half a teaspoonful of salt.

Stew twenty minutes before adding a heaping tablespoonful of butter, one teaspoonful of white sugar (for a dozen large tomatoes) and a little pepper. Stew gently fifteen minutes, and serve.

Scalloped Tomatoes.

Scald, skin, and cut each crosswise, into two or three pieces. *Just* melt a teaspoonful of butter in a pie-plate, or pudding-dish, and put into this a layer of tomatoes. Lay a bit of butter on each slice, sprinkle lightly with salt, pepper, and white sugar, and cover with fine dry cracker, or bread crumbs. Fill the dish with alternate layers of tomato crumbs, having a thick coating of crumbs on the top, and sticking tiny "dabs" of butter all over it.

Bake, covered, half an hour. Take off the tin pan, or whatever you have used to keep in the steam, and brown nicely before sending to table.

Beets.

Wash well, taking care not to scratch the skin, as they will "bleed" while in cooking if this is cut or broken.

Cook in boiling water an hour and a half if young, three, four or five hours as their age increases.

Drain, scrape off the skins, slice quickly with a sharp knife; put into a vegetable dish, and pour over them a half a cupful of vinegar, with two tablespoonfuls of butter, heated to boiling, and a little salt and pepper.

Let them stand three minutes covered in a warm place before serving.

Green Peas.

Shell and leave in very cold water fifteen minutes. Cook in plenty of boiling, salted water. They should be done in half an hour.

Shake gently in a hot colander to get rid of the water; turn into a heated deep dish, sprinkle with salt and pepper, and stir in fast and lightly *with a fork*, two tablespoonfuls of butter.

Eat while hot.

String Beans.

Do not cook these at all unless you are willing to take the trouble of "stringing" them.

With a small sharp knife cut off the stem and blossom-tips, then trim away the tough fibres from the sides carefully, and cut each bean into inch-lengths.

Lay in cold water for half an hour. Cook one hour in salted boiling water, or until the beans are tender.

Drain, butter and season as you would peas.

String beans half-trimmed and cut into slovenly, unequal lengths are a vulgar-looking, unpopular dish. Prepared as I have directed, they are comely, palatable and wholesome.

Squash.

Pare, quarter, take out the seeds, and lay in cold water for half an hour.

Boil in hot salted water thirty minutes for summer squash; twice as long if the "Hubbard" or other varieties of winter squash are used. Take up piece by piece, and squeeze gently in a clean cloth, put back into the empty dried pot, and mash quickly and smoothly with a wooden spoon.

Stir in a heaping tablespoonful of butter for one large squash, or two small ones.

Season with pepper and salt; heat and stir until smoking hot, then dish and serve.

Cauliflower.

Trim off leaves and cut the stalk short.

Lay in ice-cold water for half an hour.

Tie it up in a bit of white netting.

Put into a clean pot, cover *deep* with salted boiling water.

Boil steadily, not hard, one hour and ten minutes.

Before taking it from the fire, put a cupful of boiling water in a saucepan.

Wet a heaping teaspoonful of corn-starch with cold water, and stir into the boiling until it thickens. Then add two tablespoonfuls of butter, and when this is well stirred in, the strained juice of a lemon.

Remove the net from the cauliflower, lay in a deep dish, and pour over it the drawn butter made by the addition of the lemon juice into *sauce tartare*.

Egg Plant.

Slice it crosswise, and about an inch thick; lay in strong salt water for one hour with a plate on the topmost slice to keep it under the brine.

This will draw out the bitter taste.

Put a cupful of pounded crackers into a flat dish and season with salt and pepper.

Beat the yolks of two eggs in a shallow bowl. Wipe each slice of the egg plant *dry*, dip it in the egg, and roll it over and over in the crumbs. Have ready heated in a frying-pan, some sweet lard, and fry the vegetables in it to a fine brown.

As each slice is done, lay it in a hot colander set in the open oven, that every drop of grease may be dried off. Serve on a hot platter.

12
DESSERTS.

ENGLISH cooks would call this "A Chapter on Sweets." "*Dessert*" with them is usually applied to fruits, nuts, etc. Webster defines the word thus:

"A service of pastry, fruit or sweetmeats at the close of an entertainment; the last course at the table after the meat."

Without dwelling upon the fact that when fruit and coffee are served they follow pastry or puddings or sweetmeats, we take advantage of the elastic definition and assume that the dessert of the family dinner is a single preparation of "sweets."

The too-universal PIE will not appear on our *menu*. I am tempted to wish its manufacture might soon be numbered among the lost arts.

Bayard Taylor once said that "If Rum had slain its thousands in America, Pork-fat (fried) and Pies had slain their ten thousands."

The average pastry of our beloved land would drive a Patrick Henry to self-exile if he were obliged to eat it every day. Nor could one of a dozen inexperienced cooks manipulate puff-paste as it should be handled in order to be flaky and tender. Dexterity of motion and strength of wrist are needed for this operation, such as belong only to the trained cook.

The more wholesome and daintier jellies, custards and trifles, and plain puddings we have selected from the vast variety of sweet things known to our housewives, are adapted to the powers of novices in cookery, and not unworthy the attention of adepts.

Boiled Custard.

This is the base of so many nice "fancy dishes," and is itself so excellent and popular that we may properly lay the knowledge how to prepare it properly as the foundation-stone of dessert making.

One quart of fresh, sweet milk.

Five eggs.

One cup of sugar.

One quarter teaspoonful of salt.

One teaspoonful of essence of vanilla, lemon or bitter almond.

Heat the milk to a boil in a farina kettle, or in a tin pail set in a pot of boiling water.

In warm weather put a bit of soda no larger than a pea in the milk. While it is heating beat the eggs in a bowl. When the milk is scalding, add the salt and sugar, and pour the hot liquid upon the eggs, stirring all the while. Beat up well and return to the inner vessel, keeping the water in the outer at a hard boil. Stir two or three times in the first five minutes; afterward, almost constantly.

In a quarter of an hour it *ought* to be done, but of this you can only judge by close observation and practice.

The color changes from deep to creamy yellow; the consistency to a soft richness that makes it drop slowly and heavily from the spoon, and the mixture *tastes* like a custard instead of uncooked eggs, sugar and milk.

When you have done it right once, you recognize these signs ever afterward.

If underdone, the custard will be crude and watery; if overdone, it will clot or break.

Take it when quite right—just at the turn—directly from the fire, and pour into a bowl to cool, before flavoring with the essence.

With a good boiled custard as the beginning we can make scores of delightful desserts. First among these we may place

Cup Custard.

Fill small glasses nearly to the top with cold custard.

Whip the whites of three eggs stiff.

Beat in three teaspoonfuls of bright-colored jelly-currant, if you have it.

Heap a tablespoon of this *méringue* on the surface of each glassful.

Set in a cold place until it goes to table.

Floating Island.

Fill a glass bowl almost to the top with cold boiled custard and cover with a *méringue* made as in last receipt. Do not whip in the jelly so thoroughly as to color the frothed whites.

It is a prettier dish when the bright red specks just dot the snowy mass.

Frosted Custard.

Make a nice custard; let it get perfectly cold, and pile on it, instead of the whipped egg, a large cupful of grated cocoanut, sprinkling it on carefully, not to disturb the custard.

Eat with sponge cake.

Blanc-mange.

Like custard, this is the base—the central idea, or fact—of numberless elegant compounds, and is delightful in its simplest form.

One package of Cooper's gelatine.

Three pints of fresh, sweet milk.

One even cupful of white sugar.

One half teaspoonful of salt.

One teaspoonful of vanilla or other essence.

Soda as large as a pea, put into the milk.

Soak the gelatine three hours in a cupful of cold water. Then heat the milk (salted) in a farina kettle.

When it is scalding, stir in without taking the vessel from the fire, the sugar and soaked gelatine. Stir three minutes after it is boiling hot, and strain through a coarse cloth into a bowl. Let it get almost cold before adding the flavoring. Wet a clean mould with cold water; pour in the blanc-mange and set on ice, or in a cold place until firm.

Dip a cloth in hot water, wring until it will not drip, wrap about the mould, turn bottom upward on a flat dish, and shake gently to dislodge the contents.

Eat with powdered sugar and cream.

Chocolate Custard.

Five minutes before taking the custard from the fire, add to it three heaping tablespoonful of grated Baker's chocolate rubbed to a paste with a little cold milk. Stir until the mixture is of a rich coffee color.

Turn out, and when cold, flavor with vanilla and put into glasses.

Whip the whites of three eggs to a smooth *méringue*, beat in three tablespoonfuls of powdered sugar, and heap upon the brown mixture.

Chocolate Blanc-mange.

(Our French scholars will say that this should be termed "*Brun-mange.*")

Mix with the soaked gelatine four heaping tablespoonfuls of Baker's chocolate, grated, and stir into the scalding milk, and treat as above directed. In straining, squeeze the bag hard to extract all the coloring matter. Flavor with vanilla.

Coffee Blanc-mange.

Soak the gelatine in a cupful of strong, clear black coffee, instead of the cold water, and proceed as with plain blanc-mange, using no other flavoring than the coffee.

Tea Blanc-mange

Is made in the same way by substituting for the water very strong, mixed tea. Eat with powdered sugar and cream.

Pineapple Trifle.

> One package of gelatine.
>
> Two cups of white sugar.
>
> One small pineapple, peeled and cut into bits.
>
> One-half teaspoonful of nutmeg.
>
> Juice and grated peel of a lemon.
>
> Three cups of *boiling* water.
>
> Whites of four eggs.
>
> Soak the gelatine four hours in a cup of cold water.
>
> Put into a bowl with the sugar, nutmeg, lemon-juice, and rind and minced pineapple.

Rub the fruit hard into the mixture with a wooden spoon, and let all stand together, covered, two hours.

Then pour upon it the boiling water and stir until the gelatine is dissolved.

Line a colander with a double thickness of clean flannel, and strain the mixture through it, squeezing and wringing the cloth hard, to get the full flavor of the fruit. Set on ice until cold, but not until it is hard.

It should be just "jellied" around the edges, when you begin to whip the whites of the eggs in a bowl set in ice water. When they are quite stiff, beat in a spoonful at a time the gelatine. Whip a minute after adding each supply to mix it in perfectly.

Half an hour's work with the "Dover" will give you a white spongy mass, pleasing alike to eye and taste.

Wet a mould with cold water, put in the sponge and set on ice until you are ready to turn it out.

This is a delicious dessert. For pineapple substitute strawberries, raspberries, or peaches.

A Simple Susan.

Two cups of fine, dry bread crumbs.

Three cups of chopped apple.

One cup of sugar.

One teaspoonful of mace, and half as much allspice.

Two teaspoonfuls of butter.

One tablespoonful of salt.

Butter a pudding-dish and cover the bottom with crumbs. Lay on these a thick layer of minced apple, sprinkled lightly with salt and spices—more heavily with sugar. Stick bits of butter over all. Then more crumbs, going on in this order until all the ingredients are used up. The top layer should be crumbs. Cover closely, and bake half an hour. Remove the cover and set on the upper grating of the oven until nicely browned. Send to table in the dish in which it was baked.

Sauce for the Above.

Two cupfuls of powdered sugar.

Two tablespoonfuls of butter.

Half teaspoonful of mace or nutmeg.

Juice (strained) of a lemon.

Two tablespoonfuls of boiling water.

Melt the butter with the hot water and beat in, with egg whisk or "Dover," the sugar, a little at a time, until the sauce is like a cream. Add lemon juice and nutmeg, mould into a mound on a glass dish, or a deep plate, and set in a cold place until it is firm. This is a good "hard sauce" for any hot pudding.

Cottage Pudding.

Two eggs.

One cup of milk.

One cup of sugar.

One tablespoonful of butter.

Three cups of prepared flour.

If you have not the prepared, use family flour with two tablespoonfuls of baking powder, sifted *twice* with it.

One tablespoonful of salt.

Put the sugar in a bowl, warm the butter slightly, but do not melt it, and rub it with a wooden spoon into the sugar until they are thoroughly mixed together. Beat the eggs light in another bowl, stir in the sugar and butter, then the milk, the salt, and lastly the flour.

Butter a tin cake mould well, pour in the batter and bake about forty minutes in a steady oven.

Should it rise very fast, cover the top with white paper as soon as a crust is formed, to prevent scorching.

When you think it is done stick a clean, dry straw into the thickest part. If it comes up smooth and not sticky the loaf is ready to be taken up.

Loosen the edges from the mould with a knife, turn out on a plate, and send hot to table. Cut with a keen blade into slices, and eat with pudding sauce.

An easy receipt and one that seldom fails to give general satisfaction.

13
CAKE-MAKING.

NEVER undertake cake unless you are willing to give to the business the amount of time and labor needed to make it *well*. Materials tossed together "anyhow" may, once in a great while, come out right, but the manufacturer has no right to expect this, or to be mortified when the product is a failure.

Before breaking an egg, or putting butter and sugar together, collect all your ingredients. Sift the flour and arrange close to your hand, the bowls, egg-beater, cake-moulds, ready buttered, etc.

Begin by putting the measured sugar into a bowl, and working the butter into it with a wooden spoon. Warm the butter slightly in cold weather. Rub and stir until the mixture is as smooth and light, as cream. Indeed, this process is called "creaming."

Now, beat the yolks of your eggs light and thick in another bowl; wash the egg-beater well, wipe dry and let it get cold before whipping the whites to a standing heap in a third vessel. Keep the eggs cool before and while you beat them. Add the yolks to the creamed butter and sugar, beating hard one minute; put in the milk when milk is used, the spices and flavoring; whip in the whites, and lastly, the sifted and prepared flour.

Beat *from the bottom* of the mixing-bowl with a wooden spoon, bringing it up full and high with each stroke, and as soon as the ingredients are fairly and smoothly mixed, stop beating, or your cake will be tough.

Let your first attempt be with cup-cake baked in small tins. Learn to manage your oven well before risking pound or fruit-cake.

Should the dough or batter rise very fast lay white paper over the top, that this may not harden into a crust before the middle is done. To ascertain whether the cake is ready to leave the oven, thrust a clean straw into the thickest part. If it comes out clean, take out the tins and set them *gently* on a table or shelf to cool before turning them upside down on a clean, dry cloth or dish.

A Good Cup-cake.

One cup of butter.

Two cups of sugar—powdered.

Four eggs.

One cup of sweet milk.

One teaspoonful of vanilla.

One half-teaspoonful of mace.

Three cups of prepared flour, or the same quantity of family-flour with one even teaspoonful of soda and two of cream-tartar, sifted twice with it.

Two teaspoonfuls of baking powder will serve the same end. Mix as directed in "Practical Preliminaries," and bake in small tins.

Jelly-cake

Is made by mixing the above cup-cake, leaving out the flavoring, and baking it in "jelly-cake tins," turning these out when almost cold by running a knife around the edges, and spreading all but that intended for the top with a thick coating of fruit-jelly. Sift white sugar over the upper one or frost it.

Cream-cake.

Mix a cup-cake without spice or other flavoring, bake in jelly-cake tins, and when cold spread between the layers this filling:

One egg.

One cup of milk.

One half cup of sugar.

Two rounded teaspoonfuls of corn-starch.

One teaspoonful of vanilla or other essence.

Scald the milk in a farina-kettle; wet the cornstarch with a little cold milk and stir into that over the fire until it thickens. Have the egg ready whipped light into a bowl; beat it in the sugar; pour the thick hot milk upon this, gradually, stirring fast, return to the kettle and boil (still stirring,) to a thick custard. Let it cool before seasoning.

Frost the top-cake, or sift powdered sugar over it.

Cocoanut-cake.

Mix and bake as for jelly-cake, flavoring with rose-water.

Whip the whites of three eggs to a stiff froth.

Add one cup of powdered sugar, and two thirds of a grated cocoanut.

When the cakes are cold, spread between the layers.

To the remaining third of the cocoanut add four tablespoonfuls of powdered sugar, and cover the top of the cake with it.

Apple-cake.

Mix and bake as for jelly-cake, flavoring the dough with essence of bitter almond.

Beat one egg light in a bowl, and into it a cup of sugar. Add to this the strained juice and grated rind of a lemon.

Peel and grate three fine pippins or other ripe, tart apples directly into this mixture, stirring each well in before adding another. When all are in, put into a farina-kettle and stir over the fire until the apple-custard is boiling hot and quite thick. Cool and spread between the cakes. A nice and simple cake. Eat the day it is baked.

Chocolate-cake.

Mix and bake as for jelly-cake, flavoring with vanilla. For filling, whip the whites of three eggs stiff; stir in one cup and a half of sugar and four tablespoonfuls of Baker's Vanilla Chocolate, grated. Beat hard for two minutes and spread between the layers and on the top of the cake.

White Cup-cake.

One cup of butter.

Two cups of powdered sugar.

Three cups of prepared flour.

One cup of sweet milk.

Whites of five eggs.

One teaspoonful of essence of bitter almond.

Cream butter and sugar; add milk and beat hard before putting in the whites of the eggs. Stir in flavoring and, lightly and quickly, the prepared flour. Bake in small tins.

Frosting for Cake.

Whites of three eggs.

Three cups of powdered sugar.

Strained juice of a lemon.

Put the whites into a *cold* bowl and add the sugar at once, stirring it in thoroughly. Then whip with your egg-beater until the mixture is stiff and white, adding lemon-juice as you go on. Spread thickly over the cake, and set in the sun, or in a warm room to dry.

White Lemon Cake.

Make "white cup-cake," bake in jelly cake-tins and let it get cold. Prepare a frosting as above directed, but use the juice of two lemons and the grated peel of one. Spread this mixture between the cakes and on the top.

Sponge Cake.

Do not attempt this until you have had some practice in the management of ovens, and let your first trial be with what are sometimes termed "snow-balls,"—that is, small sponge cakes, frosted. Put six eggs into a scale and ascertain their weight *exactly*. Allow for the sponge cake the weight of the eggs in sugar, and half their weight in flour. Grate the yellow peel from a lemon and squeeze the juice upon it. Let it stand ten minutes, and strain through coarse muslin, pressing out every drop.

Beat the yolks of the eggs very light and then the sugar into them; the lemon-juice; the whites, which should have been whipped to a standing froth;—finally, stir in the sifted flour swiftly and lightly. Bake in a steady oven from twenty-five to thirty minutes, glancing at them now and then, to make sure they are not scorching, and covering with white paper as they harden on top.

This is an easy, and if implicitly obeyed, a sure receipt.

Nice Gingerbread.

Three eggs.

One cup of sugar.

One cup each of molasses, "loppered" or buttermilk, and of butter.

One tablespoonful of ground ginger, a teaspoonful of cinnamon, and half as much allspice.

Four and a half *full* cups of sifted flour.

One teaspoonful of soda dissolved in a tablespoonful of boiling water.

Put butter, molasses, sugar and spice in a bowl, set in a pan of hot water and stir with a wooden spoon until they are like brown cream. Take from the water and add the milk. Beat yolks and whites together until light in another bowl, and turn the brown mixture gradually in upon them, keeping the egg-beater going briskly.

When well-mixed, add the soda, at last, the flour. Beat *hard* three minutes, and bake in well-buttered pans.

Sugar Cookies.

Two cups of sugar.

One cup of butter.

Three eggs, whites and yolks beaten together.

About three cups of flour sifted with one teaspoonful of baking powder.

One teaspoonful of nutmeg, and half this quantity of cloves.

Cream butter and sugar, beat in the whipped eggs and spice; add a handful at a time the flour, working it in until the dough is stiff enough to roll out. Flour your hands well and sprinkle flour over a pastry-board. Make a ball of the dough, and lay it on the board. Rub your rolling-pin also with flour and roll out the dough into a sheet about a quarter of an inch thick.

Cut into round cakes; sift granulated sugar over each and bake quickly.

Ginger Snaps.

Two cups of molasses.

One cup of sugar.

One cup of butter.

Five cups of flour.

One heaping teaspoonful of ground ginger, and the same quantity of allspice.

Stir molasses, sugar and butter together in a bowl set in hot water, until *very* light. Mix in spices and flour, and roll out as directed in last receipt, but in a thinner sheet. Cut into small cakes and bake quickly.

All cakes in the composition of which molasses is used, are more apt to burn than others. Watch your ginger snaps well, but opening the oven as little as may be.

These spicy and toothsome cakes are better the second day than the first, and keep well for a week or more.

www.ingramcontent.com/pod-product-compliance
Lightning Source LLC
Chambersburg PA
CBHW080023110526
44587CB00021BA/3745